Completing

the

Puzzle

The Second Anthology by Students of
The Complete Works

Edited by Christian Foley

Published by The Complete Works
The Old Truman Brewery,
91 Brick Lane,
London E1 6QL
United Kingdom,
www.tcw.org.uk/

A catalogue record for this book is available
for the British Library

ISBN 978-0-9933303-0-8

Edited by Christian Foley
Designed and typeset by Christian Foley and
Kim Richardson
Cover image by Tola Oluwole
Printed and bound by Bookpress.eu

10 9 8 7 6 5 4 3 2 1

"This is work that deserves to be read and heard, to be appreciated for all of its angles on life, from the sharp-edged to the celebratory—and ultimately, that's what this work represents: a celebration of the power of creative self-expression, the power of an honest engagement with poetry."

- Jacob Sam-La Rose, Author of *Breaking Silence* and *Communion*

"We need poets working in education like Christian Foley. Reading this range of voices is testimony to Christian's ability to listen to his students and not let his own artistic voice interfere with what his students have to say. The poetry in these pages is raw and honest, something many long-term writers lose. Read this book and writers from all backgrounds and experiences will find the permission to activate their writing guts."

- Raymond Antrobus, *London Poetry Laureate & Educator*

We present
puzzles in paper
and puzzles in paint
pieces of people in puzzles of pain
puzzles of people in pieces of pride
pieces of power and pieces of peace
for people are puzzles
and puzzles are hard
to piece into one
so they keep us as shards
these pieces are sharp
and we point with the pen
poignant again, for we present...
pieces of love and pieces of struggle
that are fitted with hope,
we're completing
the puzzle.

Introduction from the Editor

Christian Foley, Spoken Word Educator

Children have a way of telling the truth that most adults have long lost. *Completing the Puzzle* is the second installment in our Anthology series and it is further testament to the unique power of our student's voices. Voices that are raw, uncompromising and overwhelmingly honest. The writers in this book are aged between eight and sixteen, hailing from different backgrounds, different cultures, languages, experiences and beliefs. Yet, they all possess a shared desire to express their truth.

I Am Unconditional, our first Anthology, went on to be studied by universities, showcased at literary festivals and referenced in international teaching conferences – in this respect, the words of our students were carried further than they ever anticipated. Similarly, in my introduction to *I Am Unconditional*, I wrote that it was a book that may never reach the eyes of wider society. I was wrong. I was not perhaps as wrong as one of my students in year 11 who wrote, 'I hate poetry with a passion! I have never done it! and never will!' The same student has contributed a number of poems to this project and keeps asking if the book is ready yet.

The reason that wider society listened to and read the words of our students is because our students offer a unique perspective; they do not tell us what we want to hear, but rather what we *need* to hear. Education is indeed a puzzle, and testing more, analysing league tables and instilling more rigorous exams cannot solve it. Rather, it is art and creative expression that holds the key.

Within *Completing the Puzzle* you will find a number of pieces, each one as diverse and individual as the student that created them. There is photography, there is artwork, there is prose, and there is poetry. Within this rich tapestry of themes, there are stories woven with love, with anger, with joy and with sadness.

Puzzles by their very nature are difficult to complete, some are impossible – all require patience and dedication. Compiling this Anthology has once again been an insightful process. It is a privilege to be allowed into the worlds of our students, and that they have the bravery to write these words. Reading this work is an important step towards understanding the next generation, because only through understanding, can we improve the world they will soon enter into. Piece by piece.

Foreword
Phil Richards, Founder of The Complete Works

I am honoured to write the foreword for our second anthology, *Completing the Puzzle*. This project gives a wonderful opportunity for our young people to express themselves creatively. The material in this particular edition reaffirms the reasons why we continue to publish this work for all to enjoy.

We are always seeking to find ways to empower our young people to take control of the creative process and to regain their interest in education. This anthology is a fantastic vehicle for that purpose.

The obsessive testing which unfortunately takes place in our education system at this present time, not only stifles creativity, but also communicates to young people that we are only prepared to hear the right or wrong answers to questions that we put to them. As a consequence, it is often very difficult to convince a young person that we are interested in what they have to say and will take notice and value their point of view.

This project does exactly that and it is clear that our students understand its importance. The material for this anthology is truly insightful and inspiring. These students have risen to the challenge magnificently, having the confidence to produce material that is sometimes serious, frequently poignant, often witty and always valuable!

Congratulations to all the students who contributed and my sincerest thanks to Christian Foley for his passion and dedication to this exceptionally worthwhile project.

Completing the...
Sheba Azra-Hibbert

Every morning I wake up
and add another piece to my puzzle.
The puzzle of who I am,
where I belong
and where I came from.

Music

Sylwia Buziuk

If
something
falls
into
my
ear
and
I
like
the
moral
of
it
then
that's
music.

Sapphire

Anon

The shade of sapphire set across the immense ocean, a sensational view. Crimson puddles appeared, the ocean turned into an elephantine pool of blood. The incoming tide was due, it was that time where it flushed in and slid out peacefully, but caused mass damage. The sand was soaked, our soul had been changed, the bright egg yolk sun set alight, for all to flee, the journey directs us to eternity.

The Heart and Soul of my Busy Street
Ellie-Mae Pearson

The yellow hanging lights caught my eye. The post-box red symbols painted onto the lamps popped out, a shock of colour. My eyes roamed the stalls. Sweet smells blocked my nose, images burst in my mind of international foods and celebrations. Incense sticks created smoke wisps flying towards the world's ceiling like the dragon kites being flown by hyperactive children, clutching candy and toys in their sticky, chubby fingers. I passed each stall laden with rice, sweet chickens in orange sauces, noodles and spring onions, and tightly wrapped crispy rolls packed with vegetables.

Faces smiled toothy grins; laugh lines embedded on their faces, hugging the corners of their lips. They called out to people, handing out food in silver cartons. People busily marched between stalls hunting for food that they craved to feel the sweet release of the pangs in their stomachs as their much needed morsels piled on their tongues, bursting with the various spices, sweet vegetables, grilled meats and sauces that dribbled down their chins.

They sighed and their eyes closed as they sat, clutching their make shift plates to their bodies, afraid they'd disappear and they'd have to begin the hunt again. Endless trains of the young and the old weaved between the food tables, bodies brushed against each other, eyes caught another, and smiles were given at every second.

Music led the parade; the colours and the rhythms pulsed, palpitations spreading through the bodies of anyone with ears. They were penetrated by the joyous songs and the instruments of percussion. Bodies swayed and hands clapped. People who were strangers became family in the joining of hands to dance to the music. They moved like snakes, they slithered down the street, they marched forwards, the crowd growing. Rows far back were ants, their tiny bodies were dots, you could see the colours of their clothes, their miniscule bodies creating a work of art like pointillism, splashing colour across every brick that is this road.

And they all danced. I grasped hands with a woman laden with peacock feathers. Apple green eyes climbed from her olive skin, her hazel freckles dotted her soft face across her button nose and her angular cheekbones. The blues and the greens trailed down her body and the feathers tickled her skin. She danced. This is music, and food and people. A multicultural community in love with the same things, dancing the same way, laughing the same way. This is life at its very finest.

The heart and soul of my busy street.

Step Puzzle by Frankie Batchelor

I Come From (Puzzle Piece I)
Courtney Rowden

I come from Islington
I have seen rain and cold nights most my life.

I come from watching movies and series
I come from pollution
I come from home
my home where I feel safe
where my mother makes sure I have
everything.

I come from people putting themselves on the
line
just to make sure I'm happy
I come from art and paints,
drawing and sketching.

I come from a big mainstream school
with assemblies every day
now I get searched at 9.30am.

I come from dark and cold
accompanied by hot dinners.

Islington is a place full of traffic at night
cranes worked by builders
during the afternoon.

The London Eye lights up the midnight.

I come from a place where people sing loudly
having one too many
at the Wetherspoons down the road.

I am Strong

Nathan Ottway

I am strong
but I feel so weak
I am strong
but I can't stay on my feet
I am strong
the goal I set I cannot meet
I am strong
am I setting myself up for defeat?

We are strong
have we all lost our voices?
we are strong
have we forgotten that we do have choices
we are strong
is this where we're meant to be?
rejoice in him and be set free.

He is strong
but people have taken away his confidence
he is strong
people have painted a picture of him which
just ain't true
he is strong
he wonders will he ever stop being
blue, he doesn't know what to do.

She is strong
the girls call her names
she is strong

they remove her from playing their games

she is strong
but they put her to shame

we're all strong
we need to realise
open our eyes
and see
what a difference we could make in the world
if we all just united
who cares about age, gender, sexuality, race?
Think to yourself is it worth it?
We are strong
we are who we are.

When Night Comes

Gurmita Kaur

12 O'clock... the clock strikes. It starts
the weight of your own material
teases your mind
The Ghost of Anger visits
as you coldly observe the ceiling
it lies just as awake in darkness as you do
not before long your breathing draws your
attention down-

you   stupid study
the silk covers lift with life

One O'clock
the weight on your chest is now seeping
possessing you
choked and flooding you like a memory
it is protesting to be heard!
You beg to the ceiling; unheard
the Ghost of Realisation slaps you in the face
as your eyes begin to cloud
you meet with the storm that's about to follow

Two O'clock
the eyes flicker open
the Ghost of Panic burns
at the doors of your eyes
your throat now fiercely convulses
as you lay there gasping sending your body
into reckless destruction

the hearts pleas crackle though the wind and
can be heard a mile_____ away!
Screaming in fear your lungs burn like lava
trying to feed the heart with as much as it
could steal
angry the lungs torture you
further sending you
into a state of a never ending cycle

Three O'clock
as you lay with your fingers dug into your
chest the lungs stop and the heart slows
finally you open your dry mouth taking in as
much air as you can
your body quickly consumes it and your heart
whistles a note of relief
still lying there you are greeted by The Ghost
of Sadness
feeling paper thin and dehydrated as you look
up at the ceiling
you once again feel your eyes blur
silent but strong you feel the tears dancing
making their journey down their individual
paths
you take a conscious breath once again-
but this time it sways down to your core
giving you bad butterflies

Four O'clock
the Bed stands silent and your body aches...
yawns
you stare blank-softly at the ceiling

not so painful anymore... not so Dark anymore.
The birds hum the morning melody
the ceiling is now visible-greyblue... a hybrid
of nature so beautiful, so ugly
you are comforted by The Ghost of Numbness
as you lay there- the curtains draw shut and
your eyes stop talking

the Earth now lays rich again.

My Journey to London
Keaten Boland

My Sister's boyfriend agreed to take me and my mum down to London. When we got in the car, it was jammed packed with clothes and pillows so I had to leave some things behind. When we left everybody started crying, like my friends and family for instance. As we were going I saw the horizon, I was okay until we were on the motorway. It was mayhem. The traffic was slow moving and many of the lanes were closed. The sunshine disappeared and the weather changed to thunder and lighting.

Motorbikes were trying to get past and the car drivers were trying to knock them off their bikes. It was horrendous. So my mum, my sister, her boyfriend and I went to the next junction to get something to eat but we were blocked in the Little Chef car park by two women fighting and a man trying to stop them. They were still fighting as we ordered our food and they put me off my ham and egg.

Finally we were back on track and heading to London. I got an overwhelming feeling when I saw the luminous light saying "Heathrow" on a massive blue sign. As we arrived in London it was like being in an over 18 video game. Hooligans were fighting! Cars were swooping past everyone. "OMG COULD IT GET ANY

WORSE?" said my mum. I was terrified. I couldn't wait till we got to our destination.

It got calmer as we got to West London. We passed one of the biggest tourist attractions in the country; The London Eye, looking like a big wheel with its bright lights changing colour by the hour. The HSBC Bank was even amazing for me as I lived up North before, therefore I haven't seen a bank looking so colourful, big and bright.

When we got to the destination I had Butterflies in my stomach because I was so excited that I was going to see my southern family. It had been such a long and anxious journey and I had a sense that it was going to get even worse! I was right, but it wasn't as bad as the journey. We soon reached the house and our legs were aching from having sat for so long. We went to the door, moving in a single file like penguins, our hands full with junk and baggage. We knocked on the door awkwardly.

Nobody answered; my mum and me started chuckling trying not to cry. We have been through so much stress and agony on the journey. My mum rang my auntie, whose house it was. She was out. My mum was angry. You could tell by the expression on her face that she wanted to shout, but thankfully my aunt said "The keys are under the door mat". Finally we got inside. You thought it was the end? No. They had dogs.

They were barking and were hyperactive. Yes they knew us, that's why they were so hyper. They hadn't seen us for ages, since Halloween 2012. That's long... for dogs. Finally they calmed down and helped us by putting bags in their mouth and taking it to their bed in the front room. Some people call it helping but I call it stealing. As we sat down we heard a loud bang at the door. It was the police. The neighbours called them thinking we were burglars. The police would not believe us that we had permission to be there and we couldn't reach my auntie for her to confirm. So we were taken to Crystal Palace police station.

We had to stay there for a couple hours until my auntie could be reached. As we travelled back to the house, the busy London roads were at a gridlock. I am sure I even saw two bus drivers having a fight.

Another Man's Cruel
Sywlia Buziuk

If I ruled the world

I wouldn't know what to do
I'd be so confused
should I make any rules?
I don't want to be a hypocrite
I couldn't justify it all
I can't please everybody...

One man's kind is another man's cruel.

Hackney
Bruno Job Lima

It's a beautiful, dangerous place.

Hackney.

A place with a lot of energy, fighting, death,
hands full of blood, heart full of revenge.

For power, strapped police and civilians fight
Each other...

So what's hardcore?

Hackney by Kosi Adimaly

Hackney (Part II)
Anon

The ends where nearly everyone is beefing
no face no case.

It may be all hardcore but I still miss my ex
real talk I loved her to bits

I called her last night
we had a deep talk about our relationship.

The Mystery Author

Tola Oluwole

People say you never know how much you love something until it's gone. My name is James, James Waller, and today I finally understood that saying. It started in 1982; it was my wife Yolanda's birthday. I was frustrated because I was a writer and couldn't get one of my books published, so we had no money.

I really wanted to throw her a big party that she would like, but I couldn't. Her birthday started off good but I couldn't give her that high school party, so I went out to get her a cake, when I saw a famous book publisher, Mr Grove. I greeted him and asked him if he would like to read one of my short novellas. He was hesitant at first but later read it. He told me how I have great talent but need to improve, and when I do, I should give him a ring, he gave me his card. The conversation lasted a lot longer than I bargained for.

When I got home I checked the time. It was 11.30. I was late for my wife's romantic dinner, the only time we could've shared without thinking about how we were going to pay the electric bill. I called her name but the house was as silent as a graveyard. I went in the bedroom, and there I saw her. She was silent too. I knew she was feeling despondent, it was as if she had been on the edge of a cliff, waiting for me to save her, but I didn't. I was heartbroken, how could I have been late for my love's birthday.

The next day looked brighter. I looked out on the other side of the bed but she was not there. I looked around the house and found her staring out the window, the sun was out and the wonderful birds were singing. I knew that something good was going to happen. I told Yolanda how sorry I was about her birthday and told her how couples should learn to forgive each other. She agreed.

She then added that there were my pages all over the place, and that if I wanted to get in her good books, I should clear mine up, and put them in a satchel. I set out to buy one straightaway. When I got to the pawnshop, my eyes were drawn to a particular bag, it felt like I had been put under a spell of some kind. The bag said "MJ" on it, but I couldn't fathom the reason behind the initials. I bought it anyway.

As I got home, I wanted to check the bag for any rips or tears that I may need to mend. Yet, in it, I found a paperwork book full of notes, it looked dusty and old, like it had been there for years. I read the story inside it.

It was about a man who had a son, but he could not look after his son because he was always distracted by his love of music. One afternoon the boy was playing while the man was practicing on the piano. The boy fell and slammed his head on the living room table, but the man couldn't hear over the noise of his piano.

When he walked in and saw the boy, it was a shock. He bundled him in a car and rushed him to hospital. It was too late. The man couldn't help but feel responsible. The man looked so much like his dead son that his wife couldn't bear to look at him. She left him.

I finished reading the notes. The next day I went to Mr Grove, he read them too and loved it. I told him that I wrote it. He published it. From the day, my life never stayed the same. Every newspaper and magazine wanted me to be on their cover, it was the best experience of my life, we had money, fame, anything, you could think of. There was only one problem, I didn't know how I was going to tell my Yolanda that all the money and the fame we had found, wasn't from *my* hard work.

I loved her, and I had used the money to buy her a café. I had interviews about how the book was made but I declined to comment. When I got home, I knew I couldn't continue with the lies I was telling Yolanda, so I broke the news to her about "MJ" the mystery author. She stormed out of the house, saying she needed to go for a drive. I heard the screeching of the tyres as she pulled away. Almost immediately I heard the sound of crushing metal and crackling. I rushed downstairs only to find the car on fire, burning with my wife in it. I froze. Another car had collided with her.

Everyone reaches a time where all they can do is watch something unfold, for better or for worse. I was devastated. I couldn't feel my own body. I was at the gates of hell.

At Yolanda's funeral, I swore that I was going to reveal the secret of the book and I did. Every talk show and magazine never gave me peace again. They called my phone constantly. Photographers harassed my house. Somehow the attention brought even more money. The funds in my bank account tripled. I began living off the truth.

I also began to search for "MJ" whose notes I had found. One of the newspapers tracked him down. He was an old man, a poor man that like me had lost his family. When we met, we stared at each other, channelling the pain, knowing that despite what I had done, we had a shared understanding that would last the rest of our lives. He would forgive me.

In this Life
Jeremy Boateng

In this life we experience good and bad
we meet someone special and fall in love.

Sometimes in life we lose someone
it can make us suffer for the rest of our life.

Tunnel Vision by Jeremy Boateng

Inside
Catherine Beattie

A bag in my hand often twirls
and my bottle can often leak
thoughts in my mind are troubled
and my makeup is never on point
the teeth in my mouth are all wonky
because of what people have said
I'm aiming to give up smoking
because the stress without it makes me ill
I'm scared that school will move on
without me
I don't want to be left alone
the bag in my hand is twirling
inside my bottle is leaking
now my mind is clearing
and I know I'm not on my own.

The Good Daytrip
Connor Kimpton

My name is Donny the Dog. Me and my friend Eloise, who is a dragon, arrived at the gates of Northend theme park. We didn't have any money, so I jumped onto Eloise's wings and we flew over the gate and went inside. When people saw us they were excited and scared. They screamed and ran off.

All of the rides cost £1, so we looked around for a pound. Eventually we found one on the floor by the bins. We could smell a meat smell and knew it was hotdogs. We saw a ride called Rage and sticks of rock, but what we really wanted to do was go on the Dog Ride.

The Dog Ride is a big rollercoaster. It is in the shape of a hotdog and the seats look like ketchup bottles. We asked the man who runs the ride if we could go on. He said, "only if you're well behaved. NO FIRE BREATHING!!!!!" So we gave him our pound and went on the ride.

The ride smelled like hotdog. We sat in a booth. There was no harness. The ride started. It was big and bouncy. It went 100 feet in the sky. When we got to the top, Eloise got excited and blew fire by accident. She said "sugar!" and started crying and apologised.

The ride stopped suddenly. We could smell fire. A chair was burning! Everyone was scared and crying because they couldn't get down. Then I had an idea... "Eloise can fly everyone down to safety!" Eloise got up, flew down to all the different carriages and people got on her from her head to her tail. Then she flew them down. I looked up and noticed there was one kid left at the top of the ride and hollered "Eloise, look! The kid's gonna die!"

Eloise flew up and caught him; just seconds before the whole ride collapsed. The man who owned the ride gave us a £50 reward.

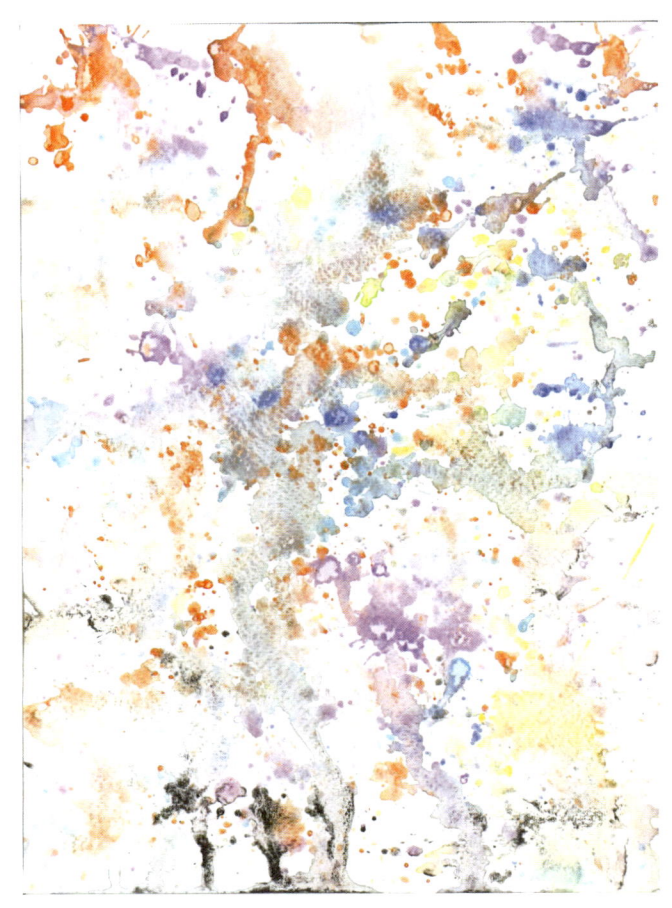

Untitled by Ryan Hogg

Animals
David Bonney

Able to take nature's hardship
Never stopping to change
Independent
Moving across the globe
Able to survive
Learning from each other
Surviving anywhere.

Our Neighbours

Anon, Emre Bilgi, Sylwia Buziuk, Romaine Williams-Reid

My neighbour above me is always playing loud music at night-time. The walls are so thin; you can hear it like it's your own house. Also when they think 'we'll rearrange the furniture' – they do it a lot. It sounds a bit like someone dropping down the stairs.

My neighbour hoovers his floor most nights at 4am. I hate this so much that I turn my music on really loud, open my window and then tape my speaker to the ceiling.

My neighbour is always stepping out his house when I'm standing outside, he gives me cold sighs, calls me various names and never apologises, smoking in the garden, throwing his leftover, unwanted cigarettes over to mine.

My neighbour is calm, he went to my Primary and Secondary School, and we always got along.

Portals
Art Fitzgerald McShane

I - *The Octopus, The Fisherman and the Fish-Tree*

The Octopus goes down to the water and the Fisherman goes through the purple portal onto the cloud.

II – *The Evil Fish-Tree Dimension*

The fisherman goes fishing and instead of a fish he gets an evil Fish-Tree. The octopus comes to save the fisherman.

III – *A Big Surprise*

The Friendly Ghost hears the Octopus through the yellow portal and comes to help. He attacks the Fish-Tree with a sword punch! The Fish-Tree is surprised to see his old brother, Friendly Ghost.

They have not seen each other since the Fish-Tree was brainwashed by King Sabada, and the Fish-Tree thought that Friendly Ghost was still in his Kingdom.

With the help of Friendly Ghost's brave royal servant, Helmet Finger, the evil Fish-Tree is overwhelmed and he flees.

IV – *The House and the Thief*

The Fisherman, the Octopus, the Friendly
Ghost, and Helmet Finger decide to build a
house, so that they can all live together. They
need somewhere big, because they are all
going to have babies!

They have lots of valuable belongings in the
house. One day, a thief comes to loot their
home and steal their stuff…

Dun-dun-DUUUUUUUUNNNN!

The Octopus suspects that the thief has been
sent by the Fish-Tree…

Dun-dun-DUUUUUUUUNNNN!

V – *The Valuable Loot*

The thief has a symbol on his chest of his suit
that represents the Fish-Tree. The valuable
loot is being stolen to build special and secret
weapons. When the thief runs off with the loot,
Helmy spots him from the top of a bush and
shoots him down with a bow and arrow.

They run outside and don't find a thief but as
they get to the wall at the back of the garden

they see the thief running into the back door where the valuable loot is.

VI – *The Chase*

"Oh my gosh! He's going through the back door!" says the octopus.
"OH MY GOSH!" says Friendly Ghost.
"What the... he tried to go out the front, but he heard us and is running to the back door!"says Helmy.

"CHASE HIM!!" they all shout at once in brouhaha.
"Oh ma goooosh..." says the thief as he's running. He goes back into the house to get his loot bag, and is chased all around it! The trio surround him completely; capture him, and decide to take him to the police station.

"Oh ma goooosh..." says the thief.

At the police station, they tell Detective Inspector Inspecty the whole story, and he cannot believe his ears.

"Oh my goodness, what a story! You're just pulling my leg though, aren't you?" he says.

"No, we're not!" exclaim the trio.

"OH MY GOSH!" shouts the Inspector.

VII – *The Attack*

Suddenly, the Fish-Tree and the minions
attack the police station! The trio split up and
attack the minions one by one and the
Friendly Ghost goes after the Fish-Tree.

The Fish-Tree and his minions retreat because
the trio are too powerful.

"Yay", they all shout.

"Take that thief," says the Friendly Ghost,
pointing at the thief.

* * * The End? * * *

Dun-dun-DUUUUUUUUNNNN! The question
mark was the real villain!

City Birds by Jeremy Boateng

Lost from Where I Belong
Hanad Salah

As I slowly open my eyes I realised. I am lost and frightened. I quickly wake up and take a minute to recognise my situation, and how I am going resolve this and get back to where I belong...

Hackney E9.

A Critical Interpretation of Poetry

Shanice Hogan

Poems are bull****
and they are there for no good.
Poetry is not going to do me nothing in my life.
I hate poetry with a passion!
I have never done it and never will!

Carnival
Caner Oruk

It was just one of those typical, boring Thursdays. It was THAT Thursday when a loud noise uprooted me out of my warm, cosy white bed.

I'm never really a morning person but today, just today I felt like I needed to jerk out of my bed to see what's going on. Usually, the view outside my bedroom window is really dull. However, it looked like a truck had spilt colourful paint all over the floors because I was not able to see the concrete. I saw people. A lot of them.

Police were everywhere. On horses and on foot like normal police officers on a normal Thursday. The people however, did not look 'normal'. They were colourful on a different level! There were: light blue, bright orange, lime green, blood red, turquoise, yellow, magenta and I could go on…

There was no space for anyone to keep moving. You either stay still or you lose your precious space. I think I had the best view to be honest. I was able to see the beginning of the carnival and also the end. I'm not going to lie but it did look blindingly fun and amazing. Who would've thought that a boring grey street like ours had the courage to start a massive, beautiful and colourful carnival?

Well, the carnival was there and was looking astonishing. The whole planet seemed to be in this carnival. I think I was the most boring and dull looking one to be honest. Everyone was looking alluring.

There was not a single fight; everyone was having the time of their lives. If you're the only person left on the planet that has not joined this boisterous carnival day, well, trust me, you're missing out big time.

Come join and see where it takes us to...

Wheels by Jasper Mcinerney

London

Courtney Rowden

Full of crime and terror
murder and stabbing
drugs and theft
this is where I live

the air is polluted
the grey smoke is all we see and smell
when we look above

teenagers locked up for multiple crimes
sirens rushing from one place
to another in minutes

petrol is what we breathe, not oxygen.

I Come From (Puzzle Piece II)
Bruno Job Lima

I come from a place
where everyone works hard
Angola.

I come from kickabouts
on the nearby estate
with goalhangers.

I come from hanging around
Mare Street and McDonalds
Hackney.

I come from hanging around with my mates,
we don't all come from
the same place.

I come from a place where the sun
shines brighter
than white gold.

I come from a place full of dreams
kids are chasing like balloons
flying on the sky.

I come from where no one
needs an alarm
as they wake up to bird sounds.

I come from Hackney now

being inspired by Christian,
my poetry teacher

to write about where I come from.

Murder on the M40
Jasper Mcinerney

Some random policeman was looking down at a corpse with a knife it it's back. "That's the third one this week" He said before falling to the ground. He landed next to the corpse as his partner stared in disbelief and horror. "That's the fourth one this week!" he said before falling to the ground, and landing next to the other corpses.

About an hour later a woman walked passed and saw the three bodies on the pavement "Oh great, that's the fifth one this week!" she said before falling to the ground next to them. This went on until there were twenty-three bodies spread across the road and causing a traffic jam all the way to Birmingham.

A guy in a car said "Crap, That's the twenty-fifth this week!" before driving away. The other drivers stuck in the line of traffic refused to turn round and instead sat beeping their horns and getting angrier and angrier. One man got out of his car and examined the bodies and found that each one had a stab wound in their back. He felt someone behind him and turned around as fast as he could. But it was too late, and as he felt a sharp knife entering his stomach, he thought, "It was supposed to be in my back, you IDIOT".

A man in the third car in the line of traffic decided he did not want to sit there any longer so he abandoned his car and walked in the opposite direction to the bodies. But a man came up to him and said, "Can you spare some change buddy? "The man was so angry and frustrated that he shoved him out of the way and carried on walking. But he regretted that as he felt a sharp knife enter his back.

A woman saw the incident out of the window of her car but could not understand what had happened - she saw the knife and the man fall but no one was holding it. When she went over to investigate, she felt a sharp pain in her back. A child in the back seat of a car saw something fly through the air shortly before the woman was killed more than twenty five meters away. The child went over to investigate, but when he tried to pick up the knife, it started floating. The child's dad got out of the car and ran over to him. Suddenly the knife flew towards him, but missed, and went flying through a nearby car window, and killing a 153-year-old man. The 153 year-old man was so old that he crumbled into a pile of dust. The dust then began to surround the knife until it was trapped. Seeing what had happened the man and his son rolled the dust covered knife up in a rug.

The next day, everybody gathered in the centre of town to see it thrown into the fire. Suddenly there's a massive explosion and loads of smoke. When it cleared, the father and son notice that everybody was dead, but not from the smoke, from stab wounds in the back.

They are the only two survivors, but for how long... THE END (To be continued? Yes? No? Maybe? Definitely... Maybe?)

Dark (Extract)
Sharman Roberts

We cannot see in the dark
or see where we are going
tracks are to be followed like trains
shiny
changing in circles.

The Ripple
Harbhajan Singh

The ghost lived in the deep water
while the moon played guitar to the sun,

the creepy birds were tweeting,
while the sun was sweeping the hot stones,

planes were happily flying through the pink
sky, while everyone was drinking tea calmly,

the birds were floating in the river,
while swans were gliding through the soft air,

a piano was calmly playing ripples,
while comets were bobbing everywhere,

everyone was getting their swimming
costumes,

while an eclipse was coming closer.

Pitch Black
Reeko Smith

Light fades to dark and back to light, and around again. The cycle continues and so I know the days are passing, but all my lights are out. Sat in my cell, wracking my brain night after night wondering what I did in a past life to deserve this. Has karma caught up with me? Death row. Convicted of a crime that I did not commit. Am I just another example of the 4% percent of the prison population sitting on death row, wondering will I ever get out of this place, or will today be the end of my story?

Three prison guards have come to my cell, I look at the time, 11am. I'm dragged out of my cell and taken to a dark room. There are no lights anywhere. They are using torches to find their way around the small room. The room only has a chair with belts put onto the armrest, and in front of the chair there is a mirror where you can see people looking at you. The guards lock me down into the chair, put my arms through the belts and pulled it 'til the blood cut off and my hands turned as purple as a beetroot.

I've been waiting in this chair of death, in total darkness for hours now. Nobody has come to check on me. Nobody cares if I'm alright or even if I'm alive. For all they know I could have broken out of this chair and made a run for it and they would never even know. I hear a noise and it is something going past my head, it is a light that is turned on, it is so bright I can't even see anymore. My mind starts to go into my past life where everything was perfect. Before all of this I had a son, I can see him aged 17 years and my beautiful wife next to him. They are stood in our £3.5 million house in London... what are they thinking while they are watching the news and seeing my face appear on TV for something I have not done? The day this crime took place that I was convicted of I was out with my family celebrating that my son passed his A-levels.

My son and wife were trying hard to prove my innocence. They spent most of their time meeting lawyers and giving them the real information, but they were all scared to act upon it. My ex-wife even said she was willing to help, but it was too late. There was not enough hours left. My time was up.

4 Hours Later...

People started entering the room in front of me. It quickly fills up with news reporters, police officers, politicians and strangers; but at the corner of my eye I notice a man that I think I recognise. He is dressed like the other reporters, but he looks just like my dad: I have not seen him for the last 25 years. I have been locked down inside of this jungle for so long, am I going mad? Is it him? I strain to see his name badge... my eyes are still blinded by the lights, but I can just about make it out.

It was a completely different name, one I do not even recognise, but I know for sure it was him. I start to move my lips, hoping to get his attention, but it was not working. Nobody can hear me in here. The three prison guards entered back into the room and they left the door open. That's when people started taking pictures of me; cameras flashing in my eye, like this was a runway shoot minus the glamour. I was sitting in the chair of death; the room was closing in on me. I looked to the left of me, a man beside me stood icily still, calmly holding the syringe that was filled with the liquid that would end my life in a matter of seconds.

The last final moments of my life all I could feel was the liquid slowly flowing through my veins it felt like a man that was in a deep amount of mud. It was a peaceful death but I had memorable moments such as when I could feel my brain and heart beat shutting down and my eyes shut close and I took my final breath and I want into a dark place where everything was pitch black

Love is Key by Tola Oluwole

Prisoner
Shanice Hogan

I choked. The smoke filled my lungs like a chimney in wintertime. The flames danced around the house and crept up every corridor. I could feel the heat rising as my skin began to burn and blister. There was no escape. This is where my story was going to end.

I was standing at the bar, I felt somebody's eyes all over me. I hadn't had any attention in a long time and I was enjoying it. He slowly approached me and in a deep, husky voice he said, "I don't know your name but excuse me miss, I saw you from across the room and you grabbed my attention, can I buy you a drink?"

I accepted his offer, by the end of the night I gave him my number. From that night we started speaking all day every day, started seeing each other three or more times a week, and before long he was calling me his girlfriend. At the beginning it was so perfect, he treated me like I was a princess, he showered me with gifts and all my friends were jealous of our whirlwind romance. They say all good things must come to an end.

As summer approached, the exams came to an end. The whole year group wanted to throw a massive party to celebrate the ending of the year and end of exams. The sun sweltered like a roaring fire and everyone was looking forward to the hottest summer that had been on record.

On the day of my final exam, he waited outside college for me in his red Vauxhall Corsa and I felt his eyes piercing through me like a dagger as I hugged and kissed my friends goodbye. "Who are they?" before I had time to explain that they were my friends from primary school, who I'd known for over 10 years, his hand connected with my face and for a minute I felt the world stop. Tears filled my eyes and the heat from my skin radiated. I remember hearing him saying sorry over and over again, saying he loved me and that it would never happen again. "I forgive you". I didn't go to the party that night.

The walls of his bedroom closed in on me during those summer months, it was suffocating. He tried to say he was keeping me to himself because he loved me so much, but I felt like a prisoner of love. My friends started calling me over twenty times a day, but I always had a new excuse. Eventually they gave up on me, could I blame them? Months later my closest friend came round to visit me. I tried to turn her away because of all the marks on my body from the fight last night, but she wouldn't take no for an answer. The bruises on my body lit up for my friend to see. "I fell down the stairs... I walked into the door". The same excuses I'd been telling people I came across. The only way I could get rid of her was to agree on going out for one night on the weekend. I knew he wouldn't be happy.

I dreaded the night out as it approached; I wore my longest skirt and top so that he couldn't complain. I sat, I chatted, I laughed, just like old times, just like the first night I met him. There was a man on the other side of the bar, he offered to buy me a drink, I accepted but told him I had a boyfriend, and that was that. I turned around and saw all my boyfriends friends standing there, they said they'd tell him about the drink. I begged and begged them not to because he'd over-react and wouldn't believe me, but I guess they didn't listen to me.

I went home that night; before I entered the house I saw the light from the living room, it glared at me like a warning sign. I should have turned around and went to my mums, but it was too late, I had opened the door. As soon as I heard his tone of voice I knew what was going to happen next, I saw my life flash. He charged at me bull-like. He started hitting me, he wouldn't stop, I felt blood streaming down my face like hot lava erupting from a volcano. As I lay paralyzed, he left the room and I thought the torture was over.

For a few minutes there was dead silence but it was interrupted by a slamming door. A few seconds later he ran past me and shot out the door like a bullet. Crackle. The smoke filled the room and the heat became more unbearable. Our whirlwind romance was over.

I Come From (Puzzle Piece III)
Sylwia Buziuk

I come from Poland
a country with a balance
of good and bad.

I come from cooking for my family
creating sensations
for their tastebuds.

I come from drawing still life
it's still more than life,
remember I'm still alive.

I come from philosophy and God
malevolence, oblivion,
the contrast of evil, pain and suffering

shaded with love, joy
and
happiness.

There's a moral in this story
just like the song's on my playlist
you know?

It's all on display like a comedian show.

Wash
Reeko Smith

It was the night, before the Henrique family was about to set off for their family trip to the United States of America. While at the family table, the second youngest child, Ka-mani, was being mouthy to his mother, Susan Brightly. As a punishment the mother demanded he was to go and sleep in the attic for the night.

Ka-mani woke up from sleeping in the attic and looked over the stairs, there was no movement coming from down stairs to his surprise. He couldn't even hear a pin drop, so he knew something had gone wrong he quickly dashed into the bathroom and washed his face, and went down to the kitchen to his amazement there was not a single soul in the house.

In a spilt second Ka-mani realised that he was left home alone, for the first time ever Ka-mani felt like a lost little lamb "how could they forget about me I'm the cute kid, the one that gets all the girls and they left me here what fools" he wanted to cry but he fought back the tears and started playing music slightly louder then he should be.

The house phone began to ring he picked it up and the person said "we are on our way young man, you can run but you can't hide from us hope you know that" the phone just cut off, Ka-mani thought it was his friends being stupid so he didn't think much of it.

A short while after, there was a knock at the door. Ka-mani slowly walked towards the front door. He noticed a strange tall figure; Ka-mani became hesitant to open the door at first. So he walked slowly to the window. Out of nowhere he saw three men coming towards the door. Ka-mani dashed up the stairs and hid in his mum's room and he just stayed there till they went away, but they didn't go, they kicked off the door and shouted "come out of hiding little man we know you're in here" they started speaking in low voices to each other and they split up and looked all over the house.

Ka-mani was curled up under the bed, with his head and legs together and his arms around them like a ball. He could hear footsteps that sounded like King Kong walking on the pavement and he was scared.

'I just want my mum', Ka-mani thought, as soon as he thought it, one of the zombies put their head under the bed, the zombie looked like the Joker, the one from the batman movie, and Ka-mani started laughing at him. But the zombie just grabbed him and pulled him from under the bed and said "I like a little bit of young fresh meat, you feel me kid" the zombie licked his lips and Ka-mani knew that it was not a joke anymore, so he started kicking the zombie but he was kicking the air and he even felt like a fool in some kind of way but he made it out of his hands and onto the floor.

Ka-mani didn't know what was going to happen next, should he run out the house or just stay?

He made a run for it. He was running around the house like a headless rooster, he went from room to room till he finally remembered that in his brother's room there were weights he could throw at the zombies, hoping they would just go away. Didn't they know he was only eight years old? So he shouted "I'm only eight years old, what could you possibly want from me I don't have anything for you, I just want to live my life and you people are stopping me, just tell me what you want please you ugly zombies?"

He did not seem to get a reply but the zombies seemed very weak, he threw one of the weights at an angle and it hit the stocky zombie in the head, and he just dropped to the floor and didn't move at all. Ka-mani was jumping like he'd just won the lottery... you know that £7.7 million feeling, well most of you won't know it because none of you have ever won it or even come close to it. Ka-mani slowly walked over to pick up another weight but it just slipped out of his hands, they were sweating like mad. He saw more zombies come out of the wall, this is like a magic show (dynamo), he thought. They came towards him, he had a feeling that they could feel the heat from his hands so Ka-mani ran over to the sink, and washed hands off. The zombies were confused. They could not smell him anymore. They sniffed the air and then stayed still and stumbled towards the door.

If only Ka-mani just knew from the start that all he had to do was wash his hands, then everything would've been fine.

This is just a lesson to be learnt in life, please just wash your hands after you do something that can cause germs.

Hand wash can kill up to 99.9% of germs per wash.

Cold
Anon

The cold is unbearable; the howling of the wind swept my ebony black hair into my eyes. I reach up to gently push it away, so much effort. My head spins and my mind rushes.

The Red Sun Rises at Dawn by Oguz Emek

The Red Sun Rises at Dawn

Oguz Emek

I awake from my own distant screams piercing through me like a bullet through red raw flesh, the screams become more and more distant and as they fade, reality seeps in.

My mind's asleep however my heart is sharply awake, I don't want to go to war but I have to, it's for my country, for my children and for my wife. I desperately reach for the letter beside my bed and clutch it close. It's the only memory that shines like a candle in the darkness; I miss my wife, my ray of light however my country needs me.

The red sun rises at dawn as the red flag whips in the wings of the wind. As I watch the flag whip, my heart fills with passion. The countdown has finally come to an end, Gallipoli 25 April 1915. As I prepare for the battle my heart pounds like the blast of an explosive cannon. As I step foot into the lifeless battlefield rubbing shoulder with my brothers, I take a wild glimpse at the flag standing tall and strong like the soldiers of this passionate country. When I stare proudly at the flag I don't see a red dyed cloth, I see a puddle of blood of my ancestors who died for me and the reflection of the half crescent moon and a star, now I'm ready to contribute to the puddle. I stand proud, I gawk freely into the far distant and watch the sunrise.

The battlefield was a nightmare; there was a strip of warm red laying across the horizon. the effect on the atmosphere was destructive and gave me a warm passionate feeling swimming through my blood. The strip of land where the tragic blood bath happened was covered in a red blanket like the warm cover that keep my people warm back home. The captain's uniforms are covered in blood blending in the scarlet uniform.

Explosions covered us like misty clouds; an eye couldn't catch an eye. I couldn't see a single being die but the distant screams scrapped my ears and left a scar in my mind.

While the red sun rose at dawn, my body collapsed, hit by a bomb, torn apart. I was a part of the few soldiers who gave up their life away for our country's glorious victory. The enemy was fighting in the sea with boats and every single soldier was still and silent, thousands of boat pieces all covered by corpses. When the bomb hit me, just before I took my last fragment of breath…

I thought to myself… Was it really worth it?

Packing (Extract from a Story)
Jfryna Ryan

The bright sun hit my window as me and my brother Junior were asleep. The smell of pancakes drifted around our room. I knew my mum was in a good mood. The door swung open and in walked mum and dad with two trays of food. Seeing that made me know that something was wrong. "Good morning" my dad said. He frightened the life out of me. My dad never talks. He then said in a loud, cheery voice "me and your mother are going on holiday!"

I was so taken aback at what he just said and asked, "Where are we going to stay?" His reply made me upset, "There's no *we*, there's just *you*... Junior's coming with us. You'll be staying at your Grandparents house".

I damn near cried at the fact I don't know them and unfortunately I was going there alone. I guess I'll have to start packing.

Expat's Lemonade
Courtney Rowden

An outsider. Not sure where I really belong. This boat is scattered with people with different stories, different pasts, stuck together like a honeycomb, but nothing sweet.

My body is a block of ice. I am a 'migrant', as cold as an ice cube in an expat's lemonade. My hands are stuck to the edge of the boat. No coat. So cold. Cold as an ice cube in an expat's lemonade.

If I was a Refugee
Emre Bilgi

I would be scared, not knowing if people will accept me or exclude me.
Except I know they won't include me.

Seeing all these posters about "migrant invasions" – that scares me.

Truly.

Arriving in Britain
Sylwia Buziuk

Confusion.

Why did they bring me here?
The fear overwhelmed me.

I heard silence in a room full of people.

Talking to a Brick Wall by Caner Oruk

If I was a refugee (Part II)
Moses Anthony-Marrah

The first thing I would see is what Britain looks like. I would smell the fried air rushing through my skin and not the smell of where I was.

I would hear how busy the streets are, people working, people asking for mercy.

Quiet

Anon

I never knew London could be so quiet. Not even the sound of a bird flapping its wings to take flight. Not even the sound of an engine roaring. Walking down the streets, it seems as though its only me in my city. The wind, stronger than anything I've ever felt, stronger than any punch I've ever taken. Sunlight marks its territory but I still can't feel its warmth.

Homeless
Bruno Job Lima

Without house
Without love
Cold and hungry.

Non-existent to the politicians
Invisible to the executives
I live on the margin,
In a corner,
Looking for a glimmer of food.

The unkindness of 'friends'.
People walking down the street
do not recognise who I am and how I live.

Homeless. Roofless.

Politicians sitting in their offices doing nothing
but still getting money.

I'm homeless with nothing.

Toeing the Line by Anonymous

I look to the Sky
Bruno Job Lima

I look to the sky
I ask for forgiveness
because if there's anyone
only God can do it.

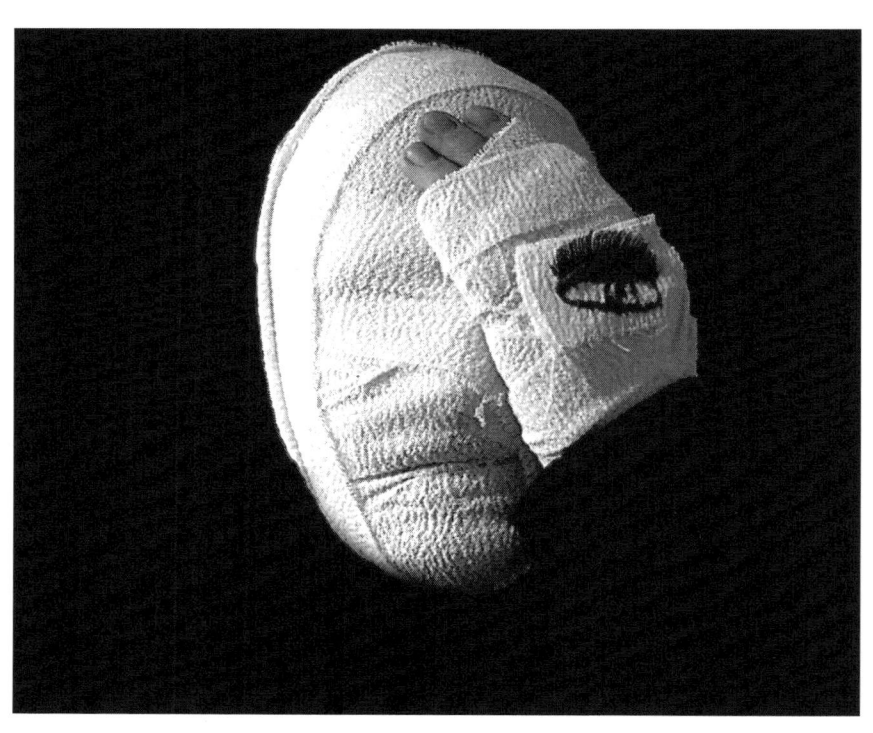

Miasma by Caner Oruk

Miasma

Ellie-Mae Pearson

I could hear them dancing behind me. Their footsteps were gunshots in my ears and I flinched each time their bare feet hit the concrete. They chanted and muttered and howled and grunted and screamed all sorts of things. They muttered low and screamed high and I couldn't make sense of a word - I don't think they were words. They just made noise. And it was deafening.

The only thing we are given

Anon

Our souls have begun to combine. We are in the same devastation. Panic is our daily routine. Served up with fear. Neglect for supper.

The only thing we are given.

God is in the TV by Dogukan Aktas

I Come From (Puzzle Piece IV)
Anon

I come from
    a tiny village in Turkey.

I come from
        where the houses
        are mud and wood.

I haven't been back since I was five.

A Time I Felt Embarrassed
Keanu McCoy

I sometimes feel embarrassed when I play football and people expect me to score or to do well. One time I thought I should do a trick shot in the goal. Someone passed me the ball and it went through my right leg and then I kicked it with my left and it went in the goal. Later in the match, I tried to do the trick again and in the same position I saw the ball coming towards me and stuck my right leg out and I tried to kick with ball with my left and it went through my legs, missed the goal and I kicked the goal keeper.

Insane
Anon

There was no turning back and nothing on the earth could bring his family back. The love he had for his family made him insane.

The Family

Shanice Hogan

She sat in the middle of the cold room
Staring at the dull walls surrounding her.

She knew it was time to leave,
grabbing her bag she heads for the door.

Does she run?
Does she scream?
Does she cry?

Or does she go and find the family she has
always wanted.

What is Family?

Courtney Rowden

Family is treasure
family is powerful
something you should keep tight
but not so tight that you fight.

it is a baby's first sight

mothers are defensive.
family is solid
family is platinum coated
with titanium, all so strong.

family is who you feel the safest with,
who you go to when you achieve
your first 5b on that literacy assessment.

family is the key I keep beside me.

family is the warmth you get
from Grandad and Grandma's fireplace
in the winter.

family is the diamond on a wedding ring,
family is golden
family is treasure
bonds are unbreakable.

Late June
Jasper Mcinerney

It was late June in the middle of a heat wave. Everyone's skin was being slowly melted by the high temperature. All the shops had sold out of fans and the air conditioning companies could not keep up with demand. All the tyres had popped and the water had evaporated, so there was nothing people could do to put out house fires, and there were a lot of them.

Jasper and Danny were sat in the kitchen at Jasper's house. Eko the (crested) Gecko's vivarium was so hot that he evolved into a salamander. Danny and Jasper were so thirsty but when they turned the tap on no water came out. Jasper decided to drink some of his own blood, because he can recycle the water in it. Danny said this wasn't a good idea and they should go to the shop. Jasper said "Ughh, FIIIINE" And they walked 125 miles to the nearest shop.

Well, that was their plan but as soon as Jasper stepped outside the door his shoe melted into the ground. Luckily, he managed to put out the fire before his other leg burned off (both burned and burnt are valid words. LOOK IT UP). If they wanted to get water they needed a better plan. So they went down to the river to pray (to the god of...????). The river was dry and flowed with fire, not water. But they saw water on the other side, and that was why they went to get Eko (he's a salamander now), to carry them across. Eko set off across the river of fire.

When they got to the other side, they noticed that it was a desert, and the water was a mirage, NOT an oasis. Danny and Jasper passed out. When they eventually woke up, they were salamanders (Hinduism was correct). They found they were actually enjoying the heat!

Then they lived happily ever after... Until the ice age came.

The Important Message

Harbhajan Singh

Tiger was feeling excited as his parcel was going to arrive. But it didn't come. So he went in his car and drove so fast that he could have crashed. But Tiger is a good driver. He went 160 mph to get to the parcel shop. He got there feeling anxious. He asked himself, "What could the parcel be?"

He waited in the queue for two hours and he was so angry and couldn't wait to open the parcel.

The man at the desk took a long time to find his parcel but he couldn't find it. So Tiger became annoyed. He shouted, "Where is my parcel?"

The manager heard Tiger and he came over. The manager said, "Hi Tiger, are you here for your parcel?"

Tiger said, "Yes."

The manager said, "Your parcel was left here by Elephant for you."

The manager gave the parcel to Tiger.

Tiger opened the parcel and there was a little message inside and it said, "SLOW DOWN".

Everything I Want
Moses Anthony-Marrah & Bruno Job Lima

If I ruled the world
I would change what we learned in school.

If I ruled the world I would make sure
the police treated everybody fairly.

If I ruled the world I would make sure
teachers let me go home when I want to

and let me do what I want to.

If I ruled the world I would want Arsenal
to win every game, cup and be first
on the table.

If I ruled the world I would love to be rich,
and have everything I want.

***

If I ruled the world, I would bring back
the smile on a vulnerable kid's face.

If I ruled the world I would work as a team
and help the young generation chase their
dreams.

If I ruled the world I would

101

build more schools all over the world
so there could be happy mothers.

If I ruled the world I would make dreams
tangible

If I ruled the world I would provide
everything for everyone

no one would be lost
my world would be beautiful.

Living on the Street (Extract)
Otto Moy

On my travels I have learned many things, just like how a life of crime doesn't really help. Even though you get food and shelter. It may be nice but not when you're getting slashed with corroded shards of metal.

The life of living on the street isn't all-bad, sometimes you get given full meals and sometimes you get a place to stay the night, you can even get on most the transport. But to be honest it's not a real life worth living. My past self is gone. My looks, strength, mind... everything.

I lay in the wet with my head having no cares about the cold, and no sense of even being alive; I live the life of a lifeless creature.

Outside Looking In by Catherine Beattie

Russian Frustrations
Catherine Beattie

Puzzling Story No. 1

The newbie bowler spoiled the joke.

Near the sunken ship, in May, working for the FBI, men were listening in to the awkward conversation being made. Suddenly the connection was lost and the men could no longer hear what was being said by the bowlers. This was an important conversation and they knew their jobs were at risk. Everyone hurried around to get the connection back. "It's the plug", said one man. "Put it back in" said another. However, the plug had vanished off the end of the cord. The men now all felt the presence of a traitor in the room.

But who was it?

Puzzling Story No. 2

The mean scout leader scribbled a note in the dark, in September, for the Russians. However, his pen stopped working. He was in the middle of a forest, what was he supposed to do? He knew that he needed to get this message across, the Russians were waiting. There was a great fluster of noise coming from the trees, a pen dropped. He looked up to the sky, more pens were now falling.

He couldn't believe what was happening, was this contact with the Gods? He picked up the pen closest to him, still slightly confused by the situation. Admiring the pen still, he placed his hand over the lid. The lid would not come off, he pulled with all his might, still nothing. He bent over for a new pen but before he could lay his fingers on it moved.

The mean scout leader then spent the night chasing pens for the Russians.

Puzzling Story No. 3

Trevor, a simple man from Bristol, was cleaning the first floor flat of the great Magnitogorsk Hotel. He knocked on room number 12 (12 out of 52 rooms he had to clean that day). With no reply, thinking the room was empty, Trevor opened the door. His eyes did not fool him, sitting in a chair before him was the most powerful man in all of Russia.

His name was Stalin. Standing behind him was an odd looking man, with scissors in his hand. This man was Stalin's hairdresser. In complete shock, the quiet man from Bristol stood. He did note move and he did not speak. The room fell silent for a good 30 seconds, until Trevor dropped a bottle of stain remover. After breaking the uncomfortable silence, Stalin's hairdresser asked for a new fruit bowl and a pair of tweezers. Trevor, still too scared to speak, gave a small nod and exited the room. The simple man from Bristol sat in the middle of the corridor, and thought about what he had just seen.

The reason I'd rather eat lemons than cat food

Connor Kimpton

The reason I'd rather eat lemons than cat food
is because you can make:
lemonade,

lemon squash,
   lemon drizzle cake,
      lemon curd,
         lemon perfume,
           lemon shower gel.

Lemons are so refreshing –
in summer you can have lemon sorbet
and take it on holiday.

Lemons are nice and buff –
and we don't get enough.
When Beyoncé's in handcuffs
she calls her new album 'Lemonade' –
and makes a mad 'ting parade!

Summer
Lamisah Morgan

The hot sun smiled down on me, scorching my face. The carnival atmosphere was electrifying as if I was a little kid again. I could hear squeals of delight from children and the sizzling of jerk chicken being cooked on a barbecue, the smell was so tantalising that it made my mouth water. Music blasted through the speakers and into the hectic crowd.

The music was like an antidote for unhappiness, the air was overpowering with such good vibes I felt like I was walking on sunshine. Nothing could ruin this moment. Exams were finally over and a weight had been lifted off my shoulders. Me and my funny, sunny friends danced together like we didn't have a care in the world. I know this day will remain unforgettable.

The carnival floats and costumes were so beautifully breathtaking; I wished I could've frozen time and lived in that sensational moment forever! The smile I was wearing at that moment was glued to my face, I felt alive again as I swung my hips to the pulsating beat, while sweat glistened on my face from the scorching hot weather; the sweet sounds of summer surged through my body like an electric shock.

The air was thick and hot, and as me and my friends moved deeper into the crowd, the smell of synthetic weave and cocoa butter infused sweat began to invade my nostrils, but not even that horrific smell could've altered my mood in that moment. For the first time this year I actually felt genuinely happen. It's amazing how a season can change your whole mood and outlook on life, isn't it?

Laughter and West Indian music filled my ears and stalls with various foods prickled my nose from the multiple different spices. I felt like I was back in Jamaica dancing on the beach when I closed my eyes, but when I opened them again, I saw the streets of West London. It felt like a dream... a good dream though.

Me and my friends wandered around, looking for a Jamaican food stall to get some jerk chicken and drinks to cool ourselves down from all the dancing we had done. The first bite I took from my jerk chicken felt like a volcano of flavour erupting on my tongue. It was shockingly spicy, but gave off a tangy taste at the same time.

The collection of different spices in my mouth instantly reminded me of the Caribbean, but suddenly the 'tropicalness' I felt in that moment began to disperse as I felt rain beginning to splatter my face lightly at first, but then it began to fall heavily. Typical English weather. I looked around me slowly watching everyone's reaction to the sudden change in weather, but everyone remained joyful and continued to dance while it rained. Summer fun has begun.

The Nine

Anon

Rolling with a shank
is not nice G
all you do is get bagged and released
then back to a trap
making bank rolls
that's all we know.

Cow Sniper by Jasper Mcinerney

A Riddle Poem
Frankie Batchelor

Trees covering the view
traps where ever you go
starvation is keen
so work as a team
eagles scoping over you
eager to get that food
rivers moving like snakes through me
the wind hissing and singing.

Dark and Stormy

Tyrese Augustus

It was a dark stormy night when
murderous thoughts coated me
like it was Winter.
The wind cried sorrowfully
busy men became lazy
the moon snuck out
women became aware that the sky had fallen
children became independent
sound itself became quiet
your home is no more
your heart is loose
the trapped were set free
and the free became trapped.
Your companions became enemies.

The City

Bradley Cole

In the city after midnight,
I'll roll round your strip on a pushbike
with the bally on its no fist fight
I got girls called Whitney and Bobby
and I send them out to the country
I'm whipping a foreign wand
and it goes o- loo real quick
do a turn and whip out the stick
chains full diamonds glistening,
£150 worth on my pinky
I don't think you're listening
I got all this money and it's shining
I go out blaming, catch an opp on the block
gonna yam him
out on late nights just grinding
we had enough of Mum crying
so I need to step up and be a man
get money and look after the fam.

My Advice for You
Anon

Care for all but accept care in return
be strong but do not take advantage
if you hold a hand, treat that as your own
hand.

Stay as an educated youth
in the best circumstances and never forget
to stay that way in the worst.

Laugh with others but keep control
never laugh after it hurts
your negatives will increase your positives

walk in small steps to take big steps
and keep the same speed
hold a rose with a delicate touch
once you pick a petal it will lose its value and
you will have killed.

Keep these words in your head but mostly in
your heart
so it pumps through your soul.

A Philosophical Question
Dogukan Aktas

If two vegetarians get in a fight with each other...

Is it still beef?

I Come From (Puzzle Piece V)
Moses Anthony-Marrah

I come from Arsenal
nearby to the Emirates,

my family support them
that's my inheritance.

I come from grime music,
it's not your music

It's my music.

I come from Stormzy, 67, Dimzy,
M-Dot (now he's in heaven)

I come from designer clothes
I'm wearing Nike, it's on sight

I keep my sights on Fifa, Black Ops
and PlayStation 4...

Mum saying what you playing PlayStation for?

I come from Empire.
I come from Gambia.
West Coast of Africa.

... Puzzle
Sheba Azra-Hibbert

Since that day
there has been a void of lost memories,
as a trueborn soldier
I got on with my life
and began to build a new one.

Acknowledgements

I would like to thank Kim Richardson of Alba Publishing for once again bringing the work of our students to the page and sharing our creative vision.

Thank you to Kayleigh Golding for her help in editing and compiling a number of the prose pieces in this book, and for her influence in helping her students to write so freely. Thank you to Chris Rosser for his help in gathering the material from our students and for the team at Head Office for the proofreading.

Thank you to Phil Richards for founding and establishing a learning environment whereby poetry, creative writing and artwork is still valued and emphasised, and for all of the tutors at The Complete Works who share this ethos. Thank you in particular to the tutors who have submitted work for this anthology and encouraged your students to do so.

Thank you to the students themselves, without whom none of this would be possible, and of course for the readers of *Completing The Puzzle* – I hope you find this work illuminating.

Index of Contributors

Index of Photography & Artwork

Completing the Puzzle